Putting on a Play

Nick Pryor

Thomson Learning
New York

Putting on a Play

First published in the
United States in 1994 by
Thomson Learning
115 Fifth Avenue
New York, NY 10003

First published in
Great Britain in 1994 by
Wayland (Publishers) Ltd.

Library of Congress
Cataloging-in-Publication Data
Pryor, Nick
  Putting on a Play / Nick Pryor.
      p.   cm.
  Includes bibliographical references (p.   )
and index.
  ISBN 1-56847-104-1
  1. Theater—Production and direction—
Juvenile literature. [1. Theater—Production
and direction.] I. Title.
PN2053.P79   1994
792'.0232—dc20   93-50765

Printed in Italy

Acknowledgments

The publishers would like to thank the
following for allowing their pictures to be used
in this book: Eye Ubiquitous 14, 16, 23, 28;
Photostage (Donald Cooper) 7 (top), 26, 27,
29, 31, 33, 41; Wayland Picture Library cover
(all), 1, 5, 6, 10, 20, 34, 37 (both), 38-39, 43.
All commissioned pictures are from the
Wayland Picture Library (APM Studios). The
text on page 24 is from Hoff the Cat Dealer
by Andrew Davies, reproduced by kind
permission of Methuen Children's Books Ltd.
Color illustrations by Peter Parr.
Diagram on page 30 by John Yates.

Contents

Words in **bold** are explained in the glossary on page 46.

A play is a story that comes alive. If you've been to a play, you know how exciting it is to see actors performing. Being in an **audience** is fun, but putting on a play is even better. You can act onstage, or you can work behind the scenes. From deciding which play you'll stage to the excitement of opening night, you'll find that it takes hard work and courage to put on a play...and you will probably love it!

This book will help you to put on a play. It will take twelve weeks if you follow the schedule here. **Curtain up!**

Different types of plays

There are many types of plays: sad plays called tragedies; funny plays called comedies; thrillers with lots of mystery and suspense; musicals with singing and dancing; science fiction plays with amazing special effects; and historical plays set in different times.

There are pictures of different plays throughout this book. Do you like some more than others?

First, tell your teacher (or scout leader or camp director) that you want to stage a play. Next, hold a meeting with other people who want to help with the play. Bring a notepad, pen, and lots of ideas!

You can make anything happen in a play!

2 Choosing a play

What type of play?

Decide if you want to do a funny or a serious play, a musical, or a mixture of several different types. If you don't write your own play, make sure to get permission to perform the one you choose from the author or the agent. This could take several telephone calls and letters.

Where do we find plays?

List all the plays you have seen.

If you don't know many plays, look in a library or bookstore.

Ask your friends and teachers or other adults for their ideas.

Even the simplest effects can look good on stage. In this production of *Titus Andronicus*, by William **Shakespeare**, the actor is being carried on a wooden pole.

You could always choose a story or poem that you like and write your own play about it.

How long should it be?

Forty-five minutes is a good length of time for an audience to enjoy a play; if it is any longer than this you will probably need an **intermission**. If you find a play that you like but it is too long, you may be able to **cut** parts of it without changing the story. You might need to ask an adult to help you with this.

If lots of people want to get involved, you could put on a big musical, like Bubbling Brown Sugar.

How many people should be in it?

How many people want to be in your play? There is no point in planning a big musical if you can get only a few actors. On the other hand, many people might want to get involved.

The **characters** in the play are called the cast. You may think there are too many or not enough parts in the cast. Don't worry; actors can double—play more than one part— or they can share a part, especially if it is a big one. This is called double casting.

Where can we perform it?

Decide where you are going to put on the play. Will it be in the school auditorium? On a raised stage or on the floor? Will you have any stage lighting and scenery? Could you perform the play outside? Remember to get permission to use any areas in your school.

7

ACT 3 Auditions

11 weeks to go. So now we have to choose our actors.

We'll have to hold some Auditions.

But one part is already cast ... mine!

Oh, all right, Joe! But we still have to pick the rest of the cast.

Telling people about it

Get permission to put up a poster telling people about the play and announcing a meeting for anyone interested in getting involved.

Planning auditions

At your meeting, write down the names of all the people who want to act in your play. Draw up a timetable, giving everyone a time and place to audition. At least two of you should be directors—the people in charge of all the aspects of the play.

The directors should plan the **auditions** carefully. Suppose twenty-four people audition. If you give each person ten minutes, it will take four hours to see them all! Each person should have about five minutes to audition.

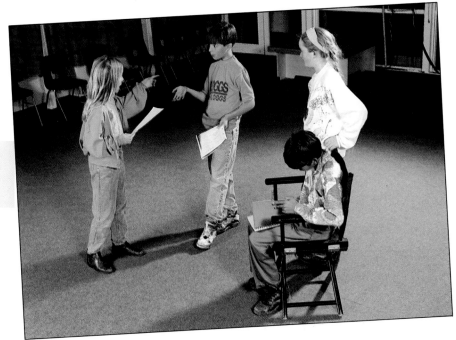

Try to make the auditions fun for everyone.

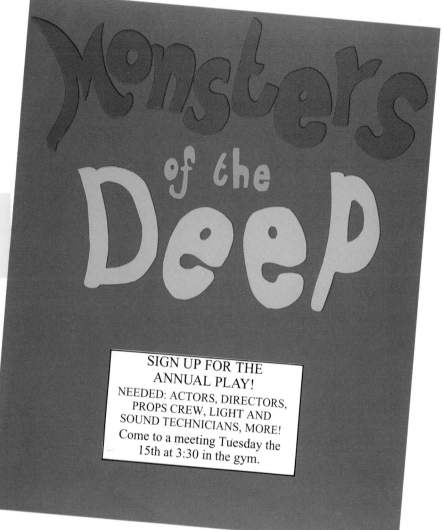

Make a bright, colorful poster to get people interested.

SIGN UP FOR THE ANNUAL PLAY!
NEEDED: ACTORS, DIRECTORS, PROPS CREW, LIGHT AND SOUND TECHNICIANS, MORE!
Come to a meeting Tuesday the 15th at 3:30 in the gym.

What happens at auditions?

At auditions, actors are often asked to read a part of the play. Doing this in pairs often helps, because it lets people relax—and also saves time. Another way is to find a short section (about twenty words) of a book or magazine for the actors to read out loud. Think about the types of characters in the play and ask each person to read as if they are those characters: as a bully; a sad person; a movie star—depending on the play you've chosen. Think about which character each person could do best.

The directors should compare notes and decide who will get parts. Auditions can make anyone nervous. Remember this when you make your decision.

Thank everyone who came to audition. If they can't all act in the play, there will be lots of other ways to take part.

Give a **script** to all the actors you have chosen.

10 weeks to go.

Right, we've got to organize things.

You mean tell People what to do?

Yes. We've got to schedule rehearsals.

And not just for the actors— we need lots of other people.

One responsible person should be the stage manager. This is a very important job. The stage manager is in charge of everything that happens on the stage during the performance. You will also need a deputy stage manager and two assistant stage managers. The stage management will have many different jobs to do during rehearsals and the play so that the show works properly.

There will be people who don't want to act but still want to be involved in the play. They can be part of the stage crew—the people who make sure everything runs smoothly.

The directors and the stage manager should meet often, to keep each other up to date with everything that happens and anything that is needed.

An eighteenth-century theater, with an ornate **proscenium** stage.

You can make a set entirely out of cardboard boxes! See the results on page 44.

Staging the play

You need to make sure that you have somewhere to perform the play when it is ready, and you must decide how you are going to stage it.

Is the play going to be on a proscenium stage, as in the picture on the left, with scenery and curtains? Would you prefer it to be in the round, when the actors perform in the middle of the audience? Or perhaps it could be an open-air performance?

If you have any ideas, draw some pictures, especially for pieces of scenery (also called the set). Discuss all your ideas, and decide which are the best, or the simplest, to make.

Organize a team of people to design and build the scenery. They need to start early, to make sure it is ready in time. Sets can be made out of almost anything: wood, paper, or painted cardboard boxes, for example. Make a model stage to help you with your design.

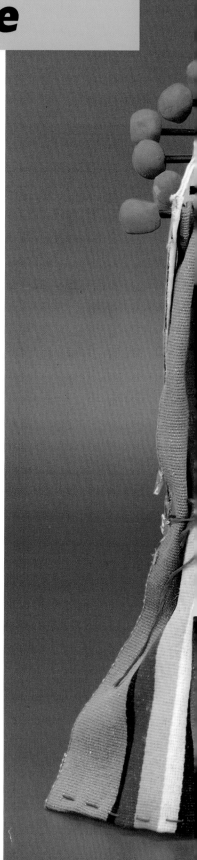

You will need:

- A large, strong cardboard box that is roughly the same shape as your actual stage.
- Lots of stiff white cardboard
- Scissors
- A ruler

- Strong glue
- Modeling clay
- Pens and pencils
- Paints and brushes
- Pieces of material
- Some long plant sticks

1. Paint the box white and turn it on its side. Cut out the top of the box, so the roof is open.

2. Your school stage will probably have curtains hanging from the ceiling to hide the **wings** and the back wall. You can make models of these by hanging the material on long plant sticks and resting them across the top of the box. If your set is going to have things hanging from the ceiling, use plant sticks to support these as well.

3. Using the stiff cardboard, make models of your pieces of scenery and put them in position. Stick a small blob of modeling clay on the back of each piece to make it stand up. You can paint the scenery with the designs you will be using on the real set.

Now you can see how your stage will look. Try moving the pieces around, to see how you could change the set during the play. Make pieces of furniture and model people out of cardboard to complete the effect.

Your model stage will be very useful to everyone. Use it to help you design, stage, and direct the play (see page 30).

The props team must get to work early, as some props can take a long time to make.

You will need at least two people to be in charge of props. Anything that is used by the actors during the play is called a prop (or property). A character might read a book, open a box, water a plant—all these objects are props and will have to be collected or made before the performance.

The props people should read through the play as soon as they can, make a list of props that will be needed, and start finding them. More props will probably be added later, so the props people should get to work right away.

Some props can be quite unusual and hard to find. This means that you may have to make them yourselves. With a little imagination you can make anything—even a butterfly net!

Make a butterfly net

—to catch humans, not butterflies!

You will need:
- A broom handle or wooden pole
- A long piece of an old garden hose
- One yard of plain net curtain
- Strong packing tape
- A needle and thread
- Scissors

2. Paint and decorate the handle.

1. Bend the garden hose into a circle, overlapping the ends, and fasten with tape. Push the broom handle into the open end of the hose and bind with more tape.

3. Cut the curtain into a cone shape so that the wide end fits around the hose. Fold the curtain in half and sew it up from the pointed end, leaving the wide end open. Fold the wide end of the curtain over the hose, and sew it up.

When making props, keep safety in mind.

15

Costumes and makeup

At least two people should take charge of the costumes, the clothes that the actors wear in the play.

You will have to read the script carefully and decide what each character might wear. Later on, you can use suggestions from the actors.

Costumes don't always have to be complicated, but if you need special costumes there are several ways to find them. Find out if your school has any old costumes in storage. Ask the actors if they have anything that can be used. Adults can also be very helpful if you need to find or make anything.

You could always try **stylized** costumes, which can be very simple. For example, the actors could wear all black or all white, unusual makeup, or colorful masks, which are easy and fun to make.

Some costumes can be very elaborate.

Makeup

You probably won't need to use a lot of makeup, but everyone should wear a little: bright lights can make skin look washed out.

Decide how the character should look and experiment with makeup.

How to make yourself look old

You will need:
• Some pale foundation
• A gray eyeliner
• White or light gray **greasepaint** or face paints
• Some pale face powder

1. Cover your face with foundation to make yourself look pale.
2. Highlight your eyes with eyeliner.
3. Looking in a mirror, frown, and trace the lines on your forehead and at the sides of your mouth with the eyeliner.
4. Put a few streaks of white or gray greasepaint in your hair and on your eyebrows, and blend it in.
5. Lightly dust some powder over your face, to keep your makeup in place.
6. Make up your hands and neck the same way.

Experiment with makeup for all of the characters in the play.

Make a mask

You will need:
- A roll of brown, gummed tape
- Tissue paper
- A saucer of water
- Scissors
- A thin rubber band
- Paints
- Glue
- Colored yarn and other odds and ends to decorate

1. Cover the actor's head with tissue paper.

2. Tear the tape into strips about 12 inches and 6 inches long.

3. Run each strip through the water then place it over the face, from the forehead to the chin.

4. Use long and short strips to fill up any gaps. The more tape you put on, the stronger the mask will be. Take extra care to make the nose, forehead, and upper lip very strong. Remember to leave a breathing gap for the actor!

5. When the face is covered, use your thumbs to gently press the tape to form shapes around the eyes, nose, and mouth.

6. Carefully remove the mask and let it dry for about two hours.

7. When it is completely dry, you can cut eyeholes, a shape for the mouth, and small holes in the nose to breathe through.

8. Paint and decorate the mask, and write the actor's name on the inside.
9. Make two small holes on either side of the mask. Thread the rubber band through the holes and tie it tightly around the back of the actor's head.

The technical crew is in charge of lighting and sound. Your play will benefit from good lighting and sound.

Lighting

You need only flashlights to create dramatic effects like this.

Big theaters have complicated lighting systems with lots of lights. These are often controlled by a computer and can create amazing effects on the stage.

There are many different kinds of lights, but the two main types are:

Spotlights
These create narrow beams of light that focus on only one or two people at a time.

Floodlights
These cover the whole stage with light.

You can change the color of a light by using **gels**.

If you are in charge of lighting, ask an adult to show you how to operate your school's lighting system. There are also many effects you can create yourself.

Flashlights can make wonderful effects on the stage. Make them different colors by sticking on gels.

If you are using ordinary overhead lights, put in colored bulbs to create unusual effects.

You must have an adult with you at all times when you are working with technical equipment.

Sound

There are three different types of sound you can use:

Live sound
Will the school orchestra, band, or musicians be playing during the performance? Where will they sit?

Sound effects (not recorded)
These could include a door slamming or a telephone ringing. Someone will have to wait **backstage** to make this sound when it is needed in the play.

Sound effects (recorded)
Music or complicated sounds, such as a fanfare or a windy storm, are often prerecorded. You can record your own sound effects, or use prerecorded cassettes from a library or music store.

Walking in a tray of gravel sounds like someone walking up a path.

Cues
When something is supposed to happen—a light going on, a sound starting, a character entering the stage—there will be a cue. Usually, certain lines are cues. The technical crew should write down all their cues on a copy of the script.

Crackly potato chip bags can be used to make good recorded sound effects. Hold them close to the microphone and rustle them between your fingers—it will sound like a fire burning. See how many sound effects you can create using other objects.

9 weeks to go.

Well, we know our cast and crew ~ I'd say we're not doing badly.

But we haven't even started rehearsals yet. What are we going to do?

Start rehearsals! Don't be frightened of them — have fun!

You will have to spend more and more time on **rehearsals** as the first performance approaches. Your school schedule will help you organize this. You may have a drama class in school every week. It would be useful if you could also have rehearsals after school at least one day a week.

Later on you should add one or two lunchtime rehearsals to your schedule.

There will be a lot of other things to do besides rehearsing. Ask your teacher if some of these jobs can be done in other classes, such as making masks in art class. Be prepared to use some of your rehearsal time to get things ready.

The read through

The first step in rehearsals is for everyone to read the play out loud.

The directors should have already read the play several times before this read through, so they can answer any questions.

The actors should try different voices and line delivery (the way they say their lines) as they read.

The directors should discuss their ideas and plans for the play before the read through. After the read through, everyone should discuss the play.

The stage manager should come to the first read through. He or she will be in charge of the prompt copy of the play. This is the script where all the actors' moves and all technical effects and cues are written in. The prompt copy should always be brought to rehearsals and must be kept up to date.

After the read through, everyone should discuss the play and new ideas.

ACTORS   LIGHTING   SOUND

SOUND CUE
8
(CAT NOISES)

SOUND ENDS

LIGHTING CUE
12
(FLASHING LIGHTS)   SOUND
CUE 9 (CAT NOISES)

3 CATS ENTER
UPSTAGE LEFT

5 CATS ENTER
DOWNSTAGE RIGHT

LIGHTING CUE
13
(BLUE LIGHT)   SOUND ENDS

MRS HOFF MOVES
TO DOWNSTAGE LEFT

HOFF THE CAT DEALER   13

Miami Yokohama, Miami Yokohama,
Yamana yamana yamana,
Pretzel pretzel pretzel!

MRS HOFF. Is that all?

PROWLER. Believe me, lady, it's plenty. Say it too loud, you'd have
so many cats through that window you'd think your flat was made
of fur. Try it, Hoff. But *quietly.*

HOFF. I feel silly.

MRS HOFF. Oh, go on, Hoff, if it's going to make us rich.

HOFF. All right. Um . . .
Miami Yokohama, Miami Yokohama,
Yamana yamana yamana,
Pretzel pretzel pretzel!

*Cats begin to flop through the window, in ones and twos, then several at
a time.*

CATS. Miaow. Prow. Perrot. Marie!

*More and more cats come in, using any of the cries from the cat
symphony.*

HOFF. There are too many! I can't cope! Stop!

Dead silence. All cats motionless.

PROWLER. You see. They are now under the fantastic power of your
iron will.

HOFF. I don't believe you.

PROWLER. Try one.

HOFF. Let's see. You. Ginger Tom. Um . . . bark like a dog.

GINGER TOM. Row! Row!

HOFF. Amazing. Thank you, Tom.

GINGER TOM (*purring*). Rubber rubber rubber rubber.

MRS HOFF. This is all very well, but I don't see what good it's going
to do. This isn't making us rich.

Make a prompt copy

You will need:
• A copy of the script
• A large scrapbook with at least twice
  as many pages as the script
• Scissors
• Glue
• Different-colored pens

1. Cut out the pages of the script and glue them to the right-hand pages of the scrapbook.

2. On the left-hand pages, write down the actors' moves and the different cues next to the line in the script where they should happen. Use a different colored pen to write each kind of cue: blue for actors, red for lighting, and green for sound, for example.

The first rehearsal

At the first rehearsal everyone should start feeling confident—and having fun! Drama games and **improvisation** are the best ways to do this; they are great fun and can be very useful for understanding and working on the play. Drama games like "Mingle" are a great way to help people relax.

"Mingle"

Think up three sentences about yourself, such as your favorite food, the best place you have ever been, and your favorite TV show. These are the only sentences you can say during the game.

Start walking around the room in lots of different directions, mumbling "mingle, mingle, mingle." When the directors shout "Freeze," you must all stop and look at the person nearest to you. The directors then tell you how to say your three sentences, for example shouting, whispering, happy, or sad. When the directors say "Go," tell each other your sentences in this way, until the directors shout "Freeze" then "Mingle," and everyone moves around again. This game is great for relaxing and for practicing acting skills!

If you are acting in the play, you must read the script carefully and think about your character. Write out the story of the play from your character's point of view. What does he or she do in the play? What do the other characters think of him or her? What do you think your character is like outside of the play? Talk to the directors and swap your ideas.

Improvisation can really help your acting. This means it is very important that you join in. Have fun, and don't be afraid to make a fool of yourself—that's what rehearsals are for!

It is important to think carefully about your character. This actor, playing the scarecrow in *The Wizard of Oz*, uses expressions and movements that suit his character.

Dialogues

Get into pairs and pretend to be your characters. Put your characters into lots of different situations, and decide how they would behave. For example, if you are playing a penny-pinching character, pretend that he or she is a shopkeeper and the other character wants to buy something—does the customer have much chance of getting a bargain? Make up different versions of this game.

The hot seat

Pretend that your character is on a TV talk show. You must speak, move, talk, and think like your character. The rest of the actors and the directors are the interviewers and ask your character lots of questions: What is your favorite food? What are your hobbies? What do you think of other characters in the play? What do you like, and what do you dislike?

Can you tell from their expressions what these characters think of each other?

What does your character look like?

The best way of deciding how your character should look is by watching other people. For example, if you are playing an older person, look at older people and see how they move. When you are alone, try to copy what you have seen in front of a mirror. Then try it in front of the other actors and the directors.

Your character's voice is also very important. Again, the best way to build your voice is by listening to other people and copying them. Try out all the voices you can think of—high, low, soft, loud, clear, hoarse —and you will soon find one that suits your part.

This actor, in the stage version of *Thunderbirds F.A.B.*, is pretending to be a rocket. How do his movements help us to believe that he is a rocket?

Voice projection

You now know many of the things that make a good actor, but all your work will be wasted if the audience can't hear you! Here is an exercise to help you with your voice projection (how loudly you can speak).

It is important to practice voice projection, especially if you are in a musical like Carmen Jones.

Stand against a wall, look at one spot on the wall opposite you, and listen to your breathing. Start to count in your head between each breath. Start with three counts, then gradually increase the number of counts between breaths. Now count out loud, aiming your voice at that spot on the wall. Gradually get louder and louder, but never shout. Stop counting, and instead say your lines loudly and clearly to the spot, pretending that you are on the stage and the wall is the audience. Try to do this exercise in bigger and bigger rooms. By the day of the performance your voice will be loud and clear.

This is where your model stage will come in useful. Find or make lots of counters: round ones for people and square ones for furniture and scenery. Make sure that they are about the right size for your model.

The directors need to work out where the actors will move during the play. On which side will they enter the stage? On which side will they leave? Where do they move when they are on the stage? This is called blocking. Blocking uses stage directions to guide the actors. Look at the diagram below to help you with your directions. Remember—stage directions are always given from the actor's point of view.

Mark these directions on your model stage. With your set designer, go through each scene of the play and decide where things are. Will you need any chairs or other furniture? If so, where should they be placed? Use your square counters to help you visualize your ideas.

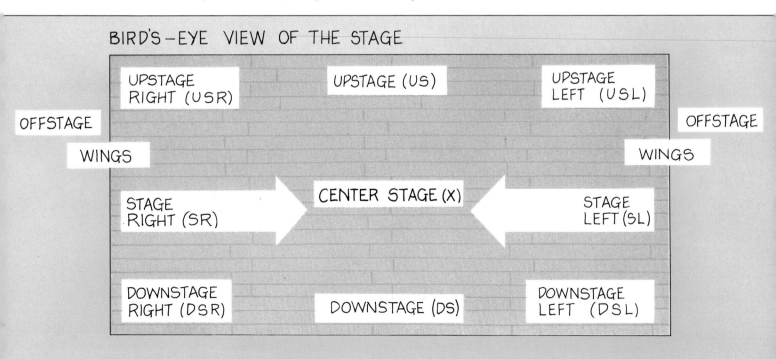

BIRD'S-EYE VIEW OF THE STAGE

| UPSTAGE RIGHT (USR) | UPSTAGE (US) | UPSTAGE LEFT (USL) |

OFFSTAGE — WINGS — OFFSTAGE — WINGS

STAGE RIGHT (SR) → CENTER STAGE (X) ← STAGE LEFT (SL)

DOWNSTAGE RIGHT (DSR) | DOWNSTAGE (DS) | DOWNSTAGE LEFT (DSL)

AUDIENCE

You will probably not be able to show some things on the stage—a backyard, for example—even if they are talked about in the script. You will have to imagine they are offstage, and decide in what direction they will be. For example, the script might say, "The telephone rings and Dorothy rushes in from the backyard." Where have you decided the yard should be? That is the direction Dorothy comes in from.

Your script will be full of clues about all this blocking. However, it will not tell you everything, and the directors and actors will have to work out a lot of blocking in rehearsals. As an example, the script might say, "Brian tries to read the paper, but he can't concentrate." Should Brian be sitting or standing? If sitting, which chair should he sit in and how should he sit? Should he pace up and down the room? The directors have to make all these decisions. The stage manager should note all the blocking in the prompt copy.

This play is being performed in the round. The audience completely surrounds the stage.

There are three important rules in blocking: 1. Don't clutter the stage. 2. Make sure the audience can see what is happening. 3. The actors must write all their moves down.

In this play, one actor pushes a custard pie into another actor's face. The whole audience wants to see this happen. Which of the photos above shows the best blocking of the scene? Why?

Learning lines

During blocking, the actors can still hold their scripts, to write down their moves. But at the same time they should start learning their lines as quickly as possible, so rehearsals can run smoothly.

The best way to test lines is by having a line run, where all the actors sit around and speak the play through without acting. The deputy stage manager should be reading the prompt copy, ready to prompt if someone forgets his or her lines. The line run will tell the cast how much they have memorized and how much more they need to do.

It is important to learn lines as quickly as possible. Some scenes, such as this one from Shakespeare's *King Lear*, are very hard to perform with a script in your hand.

13 Detailing

Now you have finished the blocking and the cast has learned its lines, the directors need to work carefully through each scene with the actors. This is called detailing. The actors should not need scripts any more, although the deputy stage manager should be ready to prompt them.

Rehearse the play in very small sections at first, then gradually build up. You will certainly want to work through the play more than once. Don't just rush through the play; if something doesn't work, then stop, go back, and try it again.

During detailing, you can start adding more movements and expressions.

Use costumes to help you change your shape!

Some sections and scenes will cause more problems than others and will therefore need more work. Sometimes you will feel a scene is not as funny or sad or exciting as it could be. There are several things you can do about scenes that need improvement:

• You might find it hard to pretend you are a big, fat man if you are small. A costume will help—just tie some pillows around your waist!

• If you want to make a scene funnier, try doing it in a really exaggerated way.

• Perhaps the scene needs more tension? Then have the actors do the scene as if they are robbing a bank and could be caught at any moment.

• If there is a language problem, for example in an old-fashioned play, try to act the scene in modern language. Use your character's version of the story to help you.

Keep working through the play until everyone knows his or her lines and moves. Once you are reasonably happy, it is time to run the play.

35

2 weeks to go.

We don't have much time — there's no way we're going to be ready!

Relax! We've got a good show and everyone is enjoying working on it ~ even you!

Don't panic! Make a checklist of where everyone is up to:

Stage management
• Are costumes and props being found and made?

• How is the set coming along? Is it being put up on the stage? Has it been painted?
• Is the prompt copy up to date?

Technical crew
• Are any recordings or special effects still needed?
• Have you arranged for all the right equipment?
• Who is working everything on the night of the play? The technical crew should come to at least two rehearsals, so they know what they have to do.

The stage management and the technical crew should now meet regularly with the directors, to make sure everything is going smoothly.

Actors
• The actors should now be running the play—practicing the play all the way through without stopping.
• When each run-through finishes, talk about the play, suggesting changes and improvements. Write all these ideas down. These are called "notes."
• Use as many of the props, costumes and pieces of scenery as possible.
• Make sure the play is the right length.

You should choose a bold design for your poster. Look at this dramatic poster for Shakespeare's *Othello*.

Japanese Kabuki actors wear stunning costumes and makeup.

New recruits

- More and more people will now want to get involved. There are lots of things for them to do.
- Posters need to be made. Perhaps you could hold a competition to design the best poster. Ask your teacher to help you make copies of the best designs. Put them up around the school and in other places, such as store windows.
- You will also want **programs** for your show. The program should tell the basic story of the play, and it should have the names of everyone involved in the production. Make sure that you spell everyone's name right, and don't forget anyone!
- You will need a **front-of-house** team, ticket sellers, and backstage helpers, as we will see later.

Costume parade

About a week before the performance all the actors should dress up in their costumes and makeup. Ask a teacher or another adult to take photos of the cast. These can be displayed in the lobby as the audience enters, or in a local newspaper article or your school magazine.

The "tech"

On the day before the first performance you must have a technical rehearsal. This is called the "tech." During the tech, the technical crew and stage management can practice all their jobs in the theater.

However straightforward your production is, the backstage team must have the chance to try out and **focus** the lights, set sound levels (how loud or soft the sound needs to be), set all the props, and then practice their cues. Each team must have a copy of the script, with a sheet numbering all their cues. The deputy stage manager should write all these numbers in the prompt copy, so that he or she can help the crew during the performance.

Remember, the tech is not for the actors. You don't need to do a full run-through of the play; just move from cue to cue. The actors should come to the tech, though, so the crew can focus lights on them and practice their cues.

In big theaters, "techs" are essential for checking that spectacular effects like these are going to work.

TECH CHECK LIST

By the end of the technical rehearsal, the crew should all know what they are doing and when:

Stage management
- All props are set on the props table.
- Offstage effects are ready.
- Someone is ready to move scenery or furniture on and off the stage.

Lighting
- Everyone knows his or her cues.
- All the lights are focused.

Sound
- All the levels are set and written down.
- All cassettes are set at the right place.

Costume
- All the actors have their own hooks or hangers for their costumes.
- Someone is ready backstage to help with costume changes.

Front-of-house
- There are tickets and programs to sell or give out.
- There are enough chairs for the audience.
- There are people to show the audience to their seats.

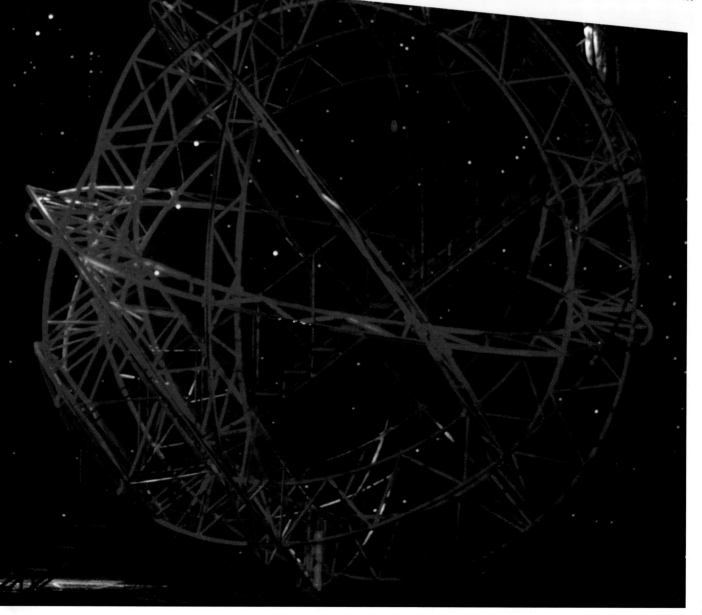

Make a props table

You will probably need two props tables to put in the wings—one for Stage Left and one for Stage Right. An assistant stage manager should be responsible for each side and will set the props that the actors need to take onstage with them.

To make a props table, you will need:
• A small table that will fit in the wings
• Some big pieces of white paper
• Tape
• A thick black pen

1. Cover the table with white paper and tape the paper down.
2. Put all the props on the table and draw around them on the white paper.
3. Write the name of each prop in its space.

Now you will always know if a prop is missing. The actors must check that all the props they need are there before the show. Props must not be touched by anyone except the assistant stage manager and the actors. After the show, return the props to the table.

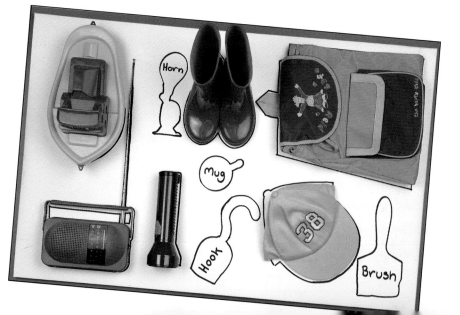

Don't forget to smile during your curtain call!

On the day or the evening before the performance, you must have the final dress rehearsal. Every part of the production should be tried in the dress rehearsal; the only thing missing here is your audience. You want your final dress rehearsal to be as close as possible to the real performance of the play.

Afterward, the directors should give the actors their last notes. You can then plan your curtain calls, or bows. Once the play has finished and the audience starts clapping, the cast should line up at the front of the stage and bow together, then leave the stage. Work out where everyone is going to stand, so the curtain call looks clean. Once you have left the stage, there might still be a lot of clapping—in that case, go out and bow all over again!

If you are still worried about anything to do with the performance, sort it out at the dress rehearsal. Tomorrow will be too late; tomorrow the show must go on! **41**

Opening night.

Our job is just about over—it's up to the actors and the rest of the team now.

You're joking! This is going to be our busiest day yet!

There will still be a lot to do on the day of the performance, but everyone should enjoy themselves—think how exciting the performance will be!

The directors should arrive first, two hours before the show, to check everything. Everyone else should arrive at least fifty minutes before the start.

Backstage

The stage manager is now in charge of the show. He or she should check that every team is ready. It helps to have an adult backstage, and remember to keep quiet! The audience will hear any noise in the wings.

Actors' nerves

All actors get nervous, even very famous ones. Don't panic; a few nerves will actually help your performance. Be friendly with your fellow actors, but don't forget to think about your part and prepare in your own way.

Give yourself enough time to prepare backstage.

In the theater it is considered to be bad luck to wish people good luck, so everyone says, "Break a leg" instead!

Warming up

Most actors need to warm themselves up before a performance. Any musicians involved will want to practice on their instruments, too.

Familiar exercises will help you to relax and give you lots of energy for the performance. Start your warm-up with some breathing and counting and the "Mingle" game. Then hum a tune, sing some scales, and do a tongue twister together.

Try this tongue twister to the tune of the William Tell Overture:

Pa's got a head like a Ping-Pong ball,
Pa's got a head like a Ping-Pong ball,
Pa's got a head like a Ping-Pong ball,
Just like a Ping-Pong ball.

Do some gentle stretching exercises.

Time calls

The stage manager is in charge of time calls. Everyone must be reminded of when the Half is (35 minutes to go), the Quarter (20 minutes to go), the Five (10 minutes) and Beginners (5 minutes, when the actors who start the show get into position).

All that's left to do now is enjoy the show!

Someone—the deputy stage manager or a teacher—should be sitting in the wings on one side of the stage reading the play from the prompt copy as it runs along. If an actor forgets his or her lines, this person will come in quickly with the right line and read it loudly and clearly enough for the actor to hear. Any other actors in the scene should also jump in with their own lines and try to cover the mistake. If something goes wrong, don't worry—think forward, not backward!

The stage manager should now run the show. The directors may be more nervous than anyone else, so they should keep out of the way! If there is more than one performance of the play, the directors should take notes.

Above all, everyone should be excited and looking forward to the performance.

So...the doors are open. Your front-of-house team is selling tickets, handing out programs, and showing people to their seats. You can hear the hubbub of the happy, excited audience looking forward to your play. The lights dim, the music starts—your play is on!

"That's a wrap"

Once you have finished the performances, you will have to strike the set (take it all down) and carefully put the props and costumes into storage. You should also make sure that the whole theater is cleaned.

Cleaning up might make you feel a little sad; after all that work, everything's over.

But remember, there is still one last thing to do: have a cast party!

Now that you've put on one play, why not do another? Try a completely different story; that way you will all learn more and the audience will see something different. Keep at it, and—who knows?—one day you could all be famous!

At the cast party.

So, do you think it went all right?

It was great! I don't know what you were so worried about!

GLOSSARY

Audience — The people who come to watch a play.

Audition — A test to choose actors for a play.

Backstage — The parts of a theater that the audience cannot see.

Characters — The people in a play.

Curtain up — The start of a performance.

Cut — Removing a part of the script.

Focus — To make the lights shine clearly and in the right direction.

Front-of-house — The people who greet the audience, sell tickets, and hand out programs.

Gels — Different-colored pieces of see-through plastic.

Greasepaint — Thick makeup used by actors.

Improvization — When actors make up lines as they go along.

Intermission — A break halfway through a performance.

Program — A list of everyone involved in a production.

Proscenium — Separated from the audience by a high arch.

Rehearsal — A practice performance of a play.

Script — A copy of a play used by an actor in rehearsals.

Shakespeare — A world-famous sixteenth- to seventeenth-century English playwright. He wrote more than 30 plays.

Stylized — Not like real life.

Wings — The offstage areas to the right and left of the stage.

FURTHER INFORMATION

Books to Read

Foley, Katheryn. *The Good Apple Guide to Creative Drama.* Carthage, IL: Good Apple, 1981.

Freeman, Ron. *Makeup Art.* Fresh Start. New York: Franklin Watts, 1991.

James, Robert. *Twenty Names in Theater.* North Bellmore, NY: Marshall Cavendish, 1990.

May, Robin. *Looking at Theater.* North Bellmore, NY: Marshall Cavendish, 1990.

Sternberg, Patricia. *On Stage: How to Put on a Play.* New York: Simon & Schuster Trade, 1983.

Wright, Lyndie. *Toy Theaters.* Fresh Start. New York: Franklin Watts, 1991.

Plays to Perform

Giff, Patricia Reilly. *Show Time at the Polk Street School: Plays You Can Do Yourself.* New York: Delacorte Press, 1992.

Landes, William-Alan. *Aladdin n' His Magic Lamp.* Studio City, CA: Players Press, 1985.

Love, Douglas. *Two Plays by Douglas Love: Blame It on the Wolf and Be Kind to Your Mother (Earth).* New York: HarperCollins Children's Books, 1993.

Kamerman, Sylvia E., ed. *Children's Plays from Favorite Stories.* Boston: Plays, 1990.

Kamerman, Sylvia E., ed. *Plays of Black Americans.* Boston: Plays, 1987.

Molyneux, Lynn and Gordner, Brad. *Act It Out: Original Plays Plus Crafts for Costumes and Scenery.* Canandaigua, NY: Trellis Books Inc., 1986.

Shakespeare, William. *Three Great Plays of Shakespeare.* White Plains, NY: Longman Publishing Group, 1991.

Thayne, Adele. *Plays from Famous Stories and Fairy Tales.* Boston: Plays, 1989.

INDEX